THE STORY OF SAGAMORE

by

Howard Kirschenbaum

Sagamore Institute
Raquette Lake, New York

ISBN 0-913393-02-9

CONTENTS

INTRODUCTION

In the latter part of the nineteenth century, the Adirondacks became one of the most fashionable tourist areas in the world. Within a relatively few years, the region moved from primitive hunting camps and boarding houses to grand hotels and a nationally unique style of architecture which came to be known as the Adirondack "Great Camp." This book tells the story of Sagamore Lodge - one of the prototypic Great Camps. Its history, peopled with generations of local families, skilled artisans and some of America's best known and wealthiest families, is a fascinating story which reveals much about America's dreams and values.

Left: *Sagamore Lake outlet.*
Above: *The "Eckford Chain" - Blue Mountain, Eagle and Utowana Lakes in foreground, Raquette Lake just visible in the distance. The setting for most of William West Durant's ventures.*

BEFORE THE DURANTS

The Adirondack Park is the largest wilderness area in the eastern United States. Its six million acres encompass an area even larger than Yellowstone, Glacier, Olympic and Yosemite National Parks combined. Although some 75 million people today live within a day's drive of the Adirondacks, the area is so wild it was not settled until the 1800s. Even the United States' western frontier was settled before the Adirondacks were thoroughly mapped and populated.

In earlier centuries, native Americans penetrated the mountain region on a seasonal basis for hunting and fishing, but left because of the long and bitter winters. The most popular theory for how the Adirondacks were named is traced to two of the native American groups who frequented the area. The Algonquin and Iroquois, warring nations, taunted one another, with the Iroquois victors calling the Algonquin "Ratiruntaks," meaning "tree eaters." The implication was that the vanquished Algonquin were so demoralized they had to survive by eating the bark off the trees. Another of the many Iroquoian pronunciations of the same word was the Mohawks' "Adirondacks," which Ebenezer Emmons, who first surveyed the area in 1837, used to describe the mountain region.

Much of the southern Adirondacks was part of a 4.5 million acre tract of land claimed by the Oneida Nation of the Iroquois Confederacy as their ancestral hunting grounds. The American patriots, eager to have Indian support in their War of Independence, promised the Oneida that after the war this land would remain theirs forever. Consequently the Oneida became the only Iroquois nation to side with the revolutionaries. After the victory, however, the New York State government repaid its allies by appropriating their lands, paying them less than one cent per acre in compensation. Three years later, in 1792, the state resold this land for over ten times that amount to a British investment company represented by speculator Alexander Macomb. The company intended to profit from land sales and agriculture, but soon went bankrupt, with Macomb and his partners never even visiting their vast Adirondack holdings.

Meanwhile, in the northern Adirondacks, 1.5 million acres, known as the "Old Military Tract," was set aside for veterans of the Revolutionary War; but few of them ever returned to claim their free land. Several other large land purchases and patents also comprised the mountain region. Consequently, most of the

Adirondacks remained undeveloped, in enormous ownership parcels, into the 1800s.

Mining companies around the turn of the century and lumber companies in the first half of the 1800s contributed to the early development and settlement in the region. They built many of the first roads into the area and railroads to its perimeter. As timber supplies to the south were exhausted, the virgin Adirondack forests fell before the lumberman's axe and saw. By 1840, major centers of logging had been established throughout the Adirondack region, which became one of the main timber suppliers to the growing nation.

The lumber and paper companies intensely exploited the Adirondacks, devastating much of the woodlands by clearcutting entire mountainsides and contributing to large forest fires. With the sun now able to penetrate through the previously lush forest canopy, the moist forest soils and mosses which previously had absorbed and steadily fed vast supplies of water downstate the year round, began to dry up. This led to soil erosion and the siltation of streams and caused the watershed to drop, seriously affecting water levels of the reservoirs and canals to the south on which much of the state depended. The lumber companies often cut over a parcel of land, stopped paying taxes, and let the land revert to the government. Then, a generation later, when a new crop of timber had matured, with friends in state and local office, they would buy back the same parcel of land from the government for a small fraction of its worth.

The public outcry over these abusive logging practices finally became so great that, in 1885, the State Forest Preserve was created to encourage the state to preserve and not sell its lands in the Adirondack and Catskill regions. In 1892, the Adirondack Park was created, delineated by a "Blue Line" on the state's map, to identify the area within which the Forest Preserve acquisitions would be concentrated. And, finally, in 1895, Article 14 (then Article 7) of the Constitution was enacted, mandating that all Forest Preserve land in the Adirondack Park be "forever wild" and never be sold, leased or traded. No one at the time dreamed that this pioneering piece of conservation legislation would threaten the existence of some of the Adirondack's most outstanding architectural resources almost a century later.

Following the lumber companies, other developers saw the northern woodlands as potential vacation lands. First rustic inns and boarding houses sprung up to meet the needs of increasing numbers of sportsmen who, often accompanied by guides, visited the region for its outstanding hunting and fishing. With the fashionable Saratoga Springs resort on its southeastern border, the Adirondacks soon saw larger hotels being built to meet the demands of the growing number of middle class and wealthy tourists reaping the rewards of the Gilded Age which followed the Civil War. In the northern Adirondacks, Paul Smith became the premier hotelier and developer, selling land to the rich and famous families who visited his hotel. In the south-central and southwestern Adirondacks, the family of Thomas Clark Durant became the leading developers and entrepreneurs.

Adirondack guide-boats on Sagamore Lake, c. 1910s.

THOMAS CLARK DURANT

Dr. Durant had left medicine years earlier to become a leading grain merchant, investor, and railroad developer. As Vice President and General Manager of the Union Pacific Railroad, he spearheaded construction of the eastern half of the first transcontinental railroad and was photographed at Promontory Point, Utah, at the famous driving of the Golden Spike in 1869.

At the same time, Durant was attempting a feat that others before him had failed to accomplish. In 1863, along with other capitalists from the New York Central and the Union Pacific railroads, Durant acquired the failing Sacketts Harbor and Saratoga Railroad Company. He intended to build a line from Saratoga Springs to Ogdensburg on the St. Lawrence River. He and his family purchased hundreds of thousands of acres, much of it at six cents per acre, along the proposed railroad route, hoping to profit from increased land values when the railroad opened the central Adirondacks to development. By 1870, sixty miles of track had been completed from Saratoga Springs to North Creek. Unexpectedly, the financial panic of 1873 led to the company's insolvency. Thus North Creek became the terminus of the Adirondack Railroad. A stagecoach line then took passengers to Blue Mountain Lake, a rough, all-day, 38 mile journey. Shortly thereafter, Dr. Durant's health began to fail, and he called upon his son to help him complete many of the Adirondack projects that he had begun.

William West Durant, c. 1884. Adirondack Museum.

WILLIAM WEST DURANT

William West Durant was on a hunting expedition in North Africa in 1873, when he received his father's summons to a family meeting in London and learned his carefree youth was about to end. William had spent twelve of the previous thirteen years in Europe, been educated in England and Germany, developed a love of architecture and engineering, and grown accustomed to associating with the aristocracy. After the Durants returned to America the following spring, William went to work selling bonds in New York City, learning the basics of business and finance.

It must have been a long journey for young Durant, psychologically as well as physically, from England to New York City to the Adirondack wilderness. To get to Raquette Lake, which he viewed for the first time in the summer of 1876, he took the train from New York to Albany, transferred to Saratoga Springs, and transferred again to his father's Adirondack Railroad to North Creek. Seven and a half bumpy hours later, William, his father, his sister Heloise, and three other members of their party, arrived at Blue Mountain Lake where the road ended. Guides rowed them by guide-boat along the "Eckford Chain" - from Blue Mountain Lake to Eagle Lake to the end of Utowana Lake. While the others walked, William, who had recently broken his leg, had to be carried by guide David Helms over the three quarters of a mile carry to the Marion River. Rowing down the river and into Raquette Lake, they came around a long peninsula, called "Long Point," which Dr. Durant owned most of, as he did much of the land for miles to the east, south and west. Possibly four year-round homes and a variety of rough cabins, shanties and campsites were visible as twenty-six year-old William surveyed Raquette Lake's ninety-nine miles of virtually undeveloped shoreline.

Although Dr. Durant actively participated until his death in 1885, William steadily took charge of developing the family's vast real estate holdings and interests in the area. The plan he eventually formulated was to sell waterfront parcels on the larger lakes to distinguished political figures, businessmen and professionals. In the more remote areas, he would sell much larger tracts, with a thousand or more acres and small private lakes, to the very wealthy. To accomplish this ambitious plan, several improvements would be needed - a better transportation system to the area, a major hotel, and a new concept for a vacation home.

In 1878, Durant developed his own stagecoach line, the "4 & 6 Overland Company," to bring passengers from the railroad terminus in North Creek to Indian Lake to Blue Mountain Lake. There he replaced the former rowboat and guide-boat service with steamers and, while the passengers walked, used ox-carts to haul the baggage across the Marion River Carry. That summer, the first of seven vessels, the Utowana, made her maiden voyage on Blue Mt. Lake. The Blue Mountain and Raquette Lake Steamboat Line, quickly became the main artery for travellers in the central Adirondacks.

The "Swiss Cottage" at Camp Pine Knot today.

Once he realized that his life and fortune would be tied to the central Adirondacks, Durant began to build a permanent "camp" there. He did this both for his family's use and to serve as a showplace - a "model home" in effect, that would attract people to the area and show that one could not only survive in the Adirondack wilderness but could do so in style. In the winter of 1876-77, he began supervising the construction of several relatively small and simple log buildings and tent platforms, on the southern shore of Long Point on Raquette Lake. Because they found a large and unusual pine knot on the shore, he named his compound "Camp Pine Knot." A second period of building beginning in 1879 reflected more elaborate, rustic designs, and a third, intensive phase between 1889-1892 contained several new buildings and additions.

At Camp Pine Knot, in an experimental fashion, the idea of the grand Adirondack camp was born. Durant did not have a single, unifying idea to begin with; rather he developed the camp over a fifteen year period, often through trial and error, combining several distinct architectural styles. As the surrounding forest offered the closest and least expensive source of material, the American log cabin provided the most obvious structural model, as did the rough, bark-sided, Adirondack lumber camps (which, in turn, were derived from the Algonquin wigwam and the Iroquois longhouse). Durant combined these indigenous styles with the Swiss chalet style that he had appreciated in Europe. The distinctive "Swiss Cottage" at Camp Pine Knot, expanded around 1882 from an earlier one-story cabin, grew into an impressive structure with a number of alpine features - the long gradually-slanting roof, the balconies and decorative railings, and the painted, exposed log ends. Surprisingly, he also borrowed some touches from the Japanese tea house style of building, then popular, as Japan had recently been opened to the West after Commodore Perry's voyage. The "Japanesque" influence, as it was called, was quite the rage then, and many Adirondack camps were soon decorated with oriental wall hangings, Japanese lanterns, fans and parasols.

Occasionally Durant expanded a building; but typically, when more room was needed, he would build a new building, so that eventually there were separate buildings that each corresponded to a room in a typical house - Durant's own cabin, a cottage for the children and their nurse, one for his mother, guest cabins, a recreation building, dining hall, a boat house and the like. Many of these were connected by covered walkways.

Not only was the *quantity* of Durant's buildings something of an innovation in Adirondack camp design, the *artistic quality* of the buildings was hitherto unknown or not popularized in the Adirondacks or elsewhere. Occasionally demonstrating rustic carpentry himself, Durant directed his skilled, though informally-trained craftsmen, guides and carpenters to create a myriad of forms and fancies using the natural materials available near the site - logs, branches, twigs, bark and stone. The result was a most pleasing array of natural forms in the buildings' structure, facades, furnishings and decorations, which quickly became the standard for Durant's and others' Adirondack building projects.

Aside from the family compound, an adjoining complex of simpler, board-and-batten service buildings and a farm complex a quarter-mile away contributed to the camp's self-sufficiency. Help's quarters, barns, workshops, storage buildings, smoke house, telegraph office, pasture and gardens were all part of the Durants' several hundred acre complex on Long Point.

The word "camp" had previously been used in the Adirondacks to describe a small cabin in the woods or by a lake, and it still retains that meaning today. But, after Durant, "camp" might also refer to a great estate of thousands of acres, private lakes, and twenty or more buildings. In the 1970s, the term "Great Camp" was coined, and while William West Durant was not the only builder of these grand estates of rustic, artistic design, he is considered the pioneer and most prominent developer of this unique architectural idiom.

The key features of an Adirondack Great Camp - a single-family camp, on a multi-building plan, set on the shore of the lake, constructed of natural materials, in an artistic fashion, with a high degree of self-sufficiency - found their prototype at Camp Pine Knot. Alfred Donaldson, the first serious historian of the Adirondacks, wrote that Camp Pine Knot "became the show place of the woods. Men took a circuitous route in order to gain a glimpse of it, and to have been a guest within its timbered walls and among its woodland fancies was to wear the hallmark of the envied."

DURANT'S NEXT PROJECTS

Durant's improved transportation system to the central Adirondacks was an essential part of his plan for developing the region. The travelers would also need accommodations when they arrived. Other entrepreneurs developed a number of comfortable inns and hotels on Raquette and Blue Mt. Lakes in the 1880s and 1890s, but Durant had much more ambitious ideas. He and his father attracted William's cousin Frederick Clark Durant to the Adirondacks, where in 1880, William may have helped in the construction supervision of Frederick's Camp Cedars on Forked Lake, another impressive camp of distinctive rustic design. Frederick, in turn, began building a grand hotel that could attract a greater number and a wealthier class of visitors, who might subsequently invest in Durant real estate. In 1882, Frederick's Prospect House, on Blue Mountain Lake, became by far the largest and grandest hotel of the central Adirondacks, accommodating some 500 guests. Modeled after the elegant Victorian hotels of Saratoga Springs, the Prospect House, with its five stories and wide verandas, was purported to be the first hotel in the world to have an Edison electric light bulb in every room. There were also hot and cold water in the bath house, a steam elevator, a bowling alley, a shooting gallery, a billiard room, a telegraph office, a barber shop, a pharmacy, and a famous two-story outhouse.

Many prominent businessmen and professionals thus were attracted to the central Adirondacks where they did purchase land and commission their own camps. On Raquette Lake, Durant supervised the construction of Camp Fairview (1879-1885) for Charles W. Durant, Jr. (Frederick's brother), and may have participated in the building of Camp Echo (1883) for Governor Phineas Lounsbury of Connecticut. Durant commissioned and donated the Episcopal Mission of the Good Shepherd (1880) on St. Hubert's Isle for the well-to-do families who were building camps on Raquette Lake and also built St. William's Church on Long Point (1891) for his Catholic employees. He married Janet Stott in 1884, daughter of Frank Stott, who owned another impressive Raquette Lake camp of the 1880s. In 1890, having recently sold the Adirondack Railway Company to the Delaware and Hudson, he invested $200,000, part of the profit, in building a luxury yacht, the Utowana, in which he crossed the Atlantic in 1891 and 1892, often entertaining European aristocracy and royalty aboard.

Back in the Adirondacks, Durant continued to build. He erected a small hotel, the Carry Inn, at the Marion River Carry, where he also built a sawmill to serve the region and his many projects. He rebuilt the dam on Utowana Lake and dredged the channels of Marion River and the Eckford Lakes to improve their navigability for his steamboats. He also shifted his attention several miles to the southwest where he owned most of Townships 5 and 6, including three lakes - Sumner, Mohegan and Shedd Lakes - located as points of a triangle, each two miles apart. He had primitive hunting camps built on Shedd and Sumner Lakes. On Mohegan Lake, in 1893, he undertook the building of his next major camp - Camp Uncas.

Durant designed Camp Uncas as his own home and spared no expense on its construction. It was said that 200 men labored for two years to complete the camp in 1895. The name was taken from James Fenimore Cooper's popular novel of the time *The Last of the Mohicans*, as were the names of two of the cabins at Uncas, Hawkeye and Chingachgook, some years later. Unlike the haphazard growth of Camp Pine Knot, Uncas was designed from the start as an ensemble of buildings, probably with professional help, and set on its own 1500 acre preserve, with a private lake, away from any of its neighbors. As he completed Uncas, he sold Camp Pine Knot to Collis P. Huntington, President of the Central Pacific and Southern Pacific railroads, an associate of his father, who had befriended the younger Durant. The next year, in 1896, he hired a crew of some forty workers to cut a new road eight-and-a-half miles through the woods from Eagle Bay to Mohegan Lake, making Camp Uncas and the other camps in the vicinity more accessible.

Between 1885 and 1900, according to Donaldson, William West Durant "enjoyed an unrivaled regency of prominence and popularity." His vision and entrepreneurial endeavors had clearly brought civilization to the central Adirondacks, and his works - steamboats, roads, camps, hotels, and churches - were visible throughout the region. The only problem was that, with so many projects going at once, Durant was steadily spending money faster than he was taking it in. He was continually in need of additional funds.

In 1895, Huntington introduced Durant to J. Pierpont Morgan, America's most powerful financier, who upon seeing Camp Uncas, fell in love with the camp and offered to purchase it. Durant declined, but eventually had to borrow money from Morgan, giving him a mortgage on the Uncas property as security. Unfortunately, the country was still in the grips of the financial Panic of 1893, one of the worst recessions the nation had ever experienced. Real estate sales were still slow and Durant was unable to fulfill his mortgage obligations. Eventually, he and Morgan reached an understanding, with the latter taking title to Camp Uncas in 1897.

Unable to hold on to Camp Uncas for financial reasons, facing an impending divorce, and in the midst of a lengthy law suit his sister had brought for control of their father's estate, one might think Durant would have known when to quit. Instead, he sold his yacht, sold tens of thousands of acres south of Raquette Lake to New York State for the Forest Preserve, sold his small camp and 1030 acres around Sumner Lake to New York's Lt. Governor Timothy Woodruff (who renamed the lake "Kora" after his wife and built the outstanding "Kamp Kill Kare" there, following the Durant architectural style), borrowed $200,000 from Huntington, paid off some of his creditors, and went on to build what is generally regarded to be Durant's grandest camp of all.

Living room at Camp Uncas, c. 1960, much as it appeared in 1895.

THE BUILDING OF SAGAMORE

Again taking a name from *Last of the Mohicans*, "Sagamore" is an Algonquin word, comparable to sachem. A wise old chief or venerated elder of the tribe would be known as "a sagamore." Completed between 1897-99, Sagamore was actually designed to be a relatively small family camp, much unlike the grand entertainment center into which it later evolved. The distinctive, chalet style, three-story Main Lodge (1897) was set on the tip of the peninsula jutting out into Shedd Lake - a mile-long secluded body of water, three miles south of Raquette Lake. It soon came to be known as "Sagamore Lake." To the left of the Main Lodge (called simply "the Lodge" or "Sagamore Lodge" then) was a small boat shed, and on the right was a dining room/kitchen complex. The Main Lodge, with its wrap-around porches, and the Dining Room were oriented toward the lake, with a view of the Blue Ridge wilderness and the Wakely Mountain range.

Primarily of frame construction, covered by half-log horizontal siding to create the appearance of a log building, the Main Lodge contained a lounge and two bedrooms on the first floor, one of which Durant used as his study; a master bedroom, other bedroom, dressing rooms, and sitting area on the second floor; and a children's bedroom on the third floor. Most of the interiors were wainscotted, the upper half of the walls covered with a patterned fabric, with "turkey red" curtains on all the windows. Animal skin rugs covered the floors, and in the Victorian style of the day, all bare spaces on tables, mantelpieces, window shelves and walls were filled with photographs, vases, bric-a-brac and artifacts of family history, travels and collectibles. This one building, with its five bedrooms, provided the camp's entire lodging capacity for Durant, his family and their guests. It followed, then, that the original Dining Room was a relatively small one, only 15 x 22, with a screened dining porch. Adjoining the Dining Room were the kitchen and pantries, a small staff dining area, a guides' room, five staff bedrooms on the second floor, and an attached ice house and small laundry.

Several hundred yards from the main family camp on the peninsula was the service complex. By 1899, it contained a caretaker's home, barn, wagon shed, woodshed, hen house, blacksmith shop, and ancillary buildings, including a root cellar adjacent to the large vegetable garden. Across the lake were a large pasture, corn and potato fields, and several farm buildings. Typical of Durant's major camps like Pine Knot and Uncas, Sagamore was an almost self-sufficient camp and farm complex.

Top: *Sagamore Lodge, c. 1900.*
Bottom: *Work wagon in front of original Durant dining room and porch, c. 1915.*

Durant oversaw his building projects with meticulous scrutiny and insisted on the best at any cost. The Main Lodge windows were specially made at the time and had to be hand-carried for miles through the woods to avoid breakage on the bumpy wagon road. Durant arrived one day to find that the porch had been built slightly out of level; he ordered his carpenters to tear it down and rebuilt it. On another occasion, he found that one stone in a fireplace had been placed incorrectly. Durant wanted the weathered side of the stone facing into the room, so it would look more natural. This time it was the masons who had to tear down their work and begin again. Perhaps some of these stories are apocryphal; Camp Pine Knot also claims the reversed stone anecdote. Nevertheless, the frequency of such accounts by many of his workers testify to Durant's exacting standards.

Richard Collins, Jr., for example, recalled the story of how his uncle John Callahan had been instructed to place an enormous set of elk antlers high in the third floor eve of the Main Lodge, under the wide overhanging roof peak. Durant arrived at camp, stood across the lawn from the Main Lodge and viewed the new rack up among the rafters over the third floor balcony. "It's not centered," he pronounced with displeasure. Callahan answered, "Well, Mr. Durant, it's awfully close." "That's not close enough," answered Durant who sent Collins and his crew up the ladder to measure the placement, where they verified that, indeed, the antlers had been a half inch off center. When called back to survey the adjusted rack, Durant is said to have commented, with a satisfied and instructive tone, "Now *that's* centered!"

Most of the decorative iron work on the property - such as the massive door locks and hinges and the ornate fireplace tools - was forged in the blacksmith shop. The many log beds and the rustic, built-in furniture were also made on the premises, carved and polished from tree trunks, branches and roots found in the woods around Sagamore. On May 1, 1900, Durant wrote that Sagamore "...has cost me a great deal more than any of the other camps I have built, and is much more elaborate in the way of gas and water works, heating by furnace as well as by fireplaces, system of draining, roads and stocking the lake with fish, than anything I before attempted."

Building on so grand a scale, when he was in dire financial straights to begin with, did not help Durant's fortunes. Nor did the culmination of his sister's law suit, resulting in a three-quarter-million dollar judgment against him. To salvage his declining fortunes, he tried desperately to accelerate his real estate sales. He began to build and sell camps on his property in the Newcomb area, forty miles to the northeast of Raquette Lake. Incorporated as the "Forest Park and Land Company," he plotted a 200-or-so-lot subdivision around Blue Mountain and Eagle Lakes, opened the Eagle's Nest Country Club, with a 9-hole golf course overlooking Eagle Lake, and hired the world famous golfer Harry Vardon for a week of exhibition matches to celebrate the opening. Then, to further improve the transportation system to the Blue Mountain Lake area, where his fate was now entrusted, he spearheaded two new railroads.

First, he got Collis P. Huntington, who himself had a personal interest in improving the transportation to Camp Pine Knot, to fund the Raquette Lake Railroad, an eighteen mile line which connected to the New York Central's Adirondack Division, that went from Utica to Malone. This enabled travelers to go from Grand Central Terminal in New York City to Albany, to Remsen (near Utica), to Clearwater (near Old Forge), to Raquette Lake, in a continuous rail trip of about twelve hours, instead of the much longer trip from the east by railroad, stagecoach, steamboat, oxcart and steamboat. At Raquette Lake, passengers would board a steamer which would take them to their hotel or camp on Raquette Lake or deliver them to the foot of the Marion River Carry.

There Durant built another railroad in 1900, the Marion River Carry Railway, which had two distinctions. It was the shortest standard-guage railroad in the world, running a total distance of three-quarters of a mile, and within three years had the wealthiest board of directors, including J. Pierpont Morgan, William Seward Webb, Harry Payne Whitney, H.E. Huntington, Reginald Vanderbilt, and other financial barons of the time, most of whom had purchased estates in the area. This tiny railroad, which further eased the transportation to Blue Mountain Lake, could even handle freight cars, which would be hauled across the lakes on barges. (Proof that the system did not always work lies at the bottom of Blue Mt. Lake today, in the form of a coal car which sank a barge in 1921.)

Unfortunately for Durant, while these developments might very well have benefited his land sales, they came too late. Durant was forced to continue liquidating his real estate holdings, sometimes at a fraction of their worth. Collis Huntington, who had promised Durant another substantial loan, died in 1900. In 1901 Durant was forced to sell "Sagamore Lodge and Preserve" for $162,500 - including 1526 acres, the entire lake, and all the buildings he had constructed. Other creditors moved in and by 1904 Durant was completely ruined.

Thereafter, he made his living selling real estate, conducting title searches, and trying unsuccessfully to begin other new ventures. In 1908, he was manager of a hotel in Newcomb, serving many of the men and women he formerly employed. He lived until age 83, a proud man of now humble means, with Annie Cotton, his second wife. He died in New York City in 1934.

Durant's study in East bedroom, first floor, Sagamore Lodge, 1899.

THE VANDERBILT YEARS

The new owner of Sagamore was Alfred Gwynne Vanderbilt, great-grandson of Commodore Vanderbilt, who had consolidated the New York Central Railroad and was one of the wealthiest men in the country. At age twenty-two, in 1899, Alfred inherited $46,575,000 from his father's estate. Sagamore was quite a contrast to the 137-room Fifth Avenue mansion and "The Breakers," Newport's largest palatial "cottage," in which Vanderbilt had been raised. Why choose deer and moose heads for interior decor when one could have Titians and Rembrandts? But to a sportsman like Vanderbilt, an Adirondack camp was a logical choice, and by now, many of the wealthiest and most prominent families in New York society had Adirondack camps.

In 1901, Alfred married Elsie French, and for the next several years, they visited Sagamore for brief stays, in all seasons, particularly around Christmas. Unlike Durant, the Vanderbilts wished to entertain at Sagamore. Toward this end, several buildings were added or expanded during the first two or three years of Vanderbilt's ownership, from late 1901-03.

The Playhouse, or "Casino", was built to serve as the social center for life at camp. Vanderbilt hired William Coulter as architect. Coulter was the most prominent builder of Great Camps in the Saranac Lake region, carrying the tradition forward to a new generation of rustic, artistic camps. Many of his buildings were larger than any of William West Durant's. He designed the Playhouse to follow the chalet-style lines of the Main Lodge. Using an impressive, vaulted, log truss system, open to the room, Coulter created a large open space, dominated by a massive fireplace at one end, its granite stone chimney rising eighteen feet to the peak of the ceiling. A large billiards table, rustic-based oak-surfaced Ping-pong table, roulette wheel and other games of chance filled the room, and a wet bar for mixing drinks was found in a small adjoining room in the rear. Hunting trophies from the Adirondacks and around the world lined the walls.

The Wigwam was constructed as a cottage for guests. Built over the waterfall and trout stream as it leaves Sagamore Lake, Wigwam was built in two stages. The original part had five bedrooms and a main lounge with fireplace. Four of the bedrooms had corner fireplaces, all connected to the same large chimney. Vanderbilt and his male guests retired to Wigwam after dinner to smoke cigars and play cards. Original oil paintings by Renoir and Remington decorated the walls.

Alfred Gwynne Vanderbilt and Elsie French, 1901-1908.

Additional dining capacity was achieved by doubling Durant's original dining room lengthwise, adding a second matching corner fireplace. The two halves of the room could be divided with a sliding glass partition which, when not in use, folded into a recess in the walls. The kitchen work area and staff dining room was also expanded. Up the hill in the service complex, a second caretaker's cottage, called "the Annex," was built probably during this period, and the barn and carriage shed were expanded for the Vanderbilt's horses and carriages.

In addition to expanding the camp for guests and staff, the young Vanderbilts anticipated a growing family. Lakeside Cottage was built as a nursery for their expected children and nurses, and was aptly named "The Incubator." The original building had four bedrooms, each opening onto a porch facing the lake. The Vanderbilts did have one child, William Henry Vanderbilt III.

Like others of their social group who had bought or built large camps in the Adirondacks, the Vanderbilts could leave New York City in Alfred's private railroad car, "the Wayfarer," dine going up along the Hudson, go to sleep for the night, and wake up early the next morning at the Raquette Lake Railroad Station. He purchased two elegant carriages for Sagamore and selected a matched team from his stables. These, complete with driver, liveryman and footman, routinely met the Vanderbilts and their guests at the Raquette Lake station.

In 1908, Elsie French Vanderbilt sued Alfred for a divorce, claiming that he had been guilty of improper behavior in his private railroad car. She maintained custody of their son, who later went on to become Governor of Rhode Island. Although he spent much of his time in Europe after the divorce, Vanderbilt continued occasionally to visit and entertain at Sagamore.

In 1911, Vanderbilt married Margaret Emerson McKim, a prominent leader of Society, recently divorced from her first husband. Her father, Captain Isaac Emerson, had invented Bromo-Seltzer and was head of the prosperous Emerson Drug Company in Baltimore. For the next several years, the couple spent most of their time in Europe - at Vanderbilt's country estate near London and travelling - and visited Sagamore only occasionally when in the United States. In 1913, however, they decided to make a major commitment to Sagamore as their primary vacation home and began an intensive two-year campaign of building expansion and infrastructure improvements. The same year, Vanderbilt purchased the neighboring Kamp Kill Kare from Lt. Governor Woodruff and, now in a position to select their neighbors, resold it in 1914 to Mr. and Mrs. Francis P. Garvan.

To better accommodate a still larger number of guests, The Wigwam was expanded in 1914 to its present configuration of nine-bedrooms, seven of which contained their own fireplace. A precise blue and yellow pattern for curtains, rugs, cushions, blankets, and even pitchers and wash basins was followed throughout the building. A semi-outdoor, two-lane bowling alley was also constructed in 1914, at the rear of the Playhouse. This presented a certain dilemma: since it was partially exposed to the weather, how could they insure that it would withstand the frost heaves of Adirondack winter? They solved this problem by pouring six feet of solid concrete under both lanes, the entire length, well below the frost line, and the alleys remain level to this day. For added comfort, a fireplace was included in the bowling alley design, and canvas curtains enclosed the building on inclement days and evenings.

As Sagamore grew, so did the Vanderbilts' family. Alfred Gwynne Vanderbilt II and George Washington Vanderbilt III were born in 1912 and 1914, respectively. When the family was at Sagamore, the children stayed in the bedroom/nursery area on the third floor of the Main Lodge, with their nurse or governess. The former lakeside "Incubator" cottage, now called the "Cabins", was thereby available for guests. Its four bedrooms, combined with the expanded Wigwam, now provided a total of thirteen guest bedrooms beyond the Main Lodge. Sagamore was gradually becoming an entertainment center.

Vanderbilt's guests occasionally were met at the station by his new (1913), 35-foot motor launch "The Alert," which would traverse the south part of Raquette Lake, and head up the South Inlet which was navigable to the corner of the Sagamore Preserve. There the coaches would meet them and bring them the remaining mile-and-a-half through the forest to Sagamore Lodge.

For additional convenience and comfort, in 1914, telephone service was brought to Sagamore, and a modern water and sewage system was installed that was as advanced for the time as any in America's cities. In 1915, a hydroelectric plant was built along the Sagamore Lake outlet about a mile from the lodge, enabling the camp to shift from the previous gas lighting to electricity. That some of the new lighting fixtures contained both electric *and* gas demonstrated a lack of complete confidence in the new electrical

Top: *Bowling alley at Sagamore, 1930s.*
Bottom: *One part of the flower and vegetable garden, c. 1910s.*
"Sagamore Lodge" is spelled in flowers, with eight-foot letters, along the crest of the hill.

system. An electrician was needed on the premises at all times to maintain the hydroelectric plant, wiring and lighting.

A larger family and greater number of guests naturally required a larger staff, so in late 1914, the foundations for two massive new service buildings - the "New Laundry" and the "Men's Camp" - were begun. The New Laundry was erected in 1915 near the old laundry and ice house. With its thick, poured concrete foundation, steel beams, and painted plaster walls over the frame construction, it was unlike any previous building at Sagamore; but its exterior bark and decorative log covering and its above-ground stone masonry made it blend into Sagamore's rustic character. The interior trim work, cabinetry and window hardware matched the excellence, if not the rustic artistry, of Sagamore's woodwork. On the first floor, the building contained a large laundry and ironing area, a staff living room with brick fireplace, linen room, sewing room, valeting room, and superintendent's office. The second floor had eleven bedrooms for staff, visiting businesspeople, and overflow guests.

In the caretaking complex, a new carpenter's shop/paint shop was built, and the hen house was relocated and expanded. These buildings paled in size next to the nineteen-room Men's Camp, another poured concrete, steel and plaster structure, although shingle style in its exterior appearance. It housed a caretaking family on the first floor, with the family's large kitchen serving an adjoining staff dining room, which in turn adjoined a staff living room. On the second floor were nine large bedrooms for additional staff. Bachelors or married men who temporarily left their families to work for the Vanderbilts would be housed here.

Attached to the Men's Camp, Vanderbilt also undertook the building of an enormous horse stables and staff recreation building. It was never completed. In May of 1915, Vanderbilt boarded a ship heading for England to watch one of his new horses compete in an important race. Reporters asked him if he feared enemy submarines, and he responded, "The Germans would not dare attack this ship." The ship, however, was the Luisitania, which was torpedoed off the coast of Ireland and sank within 20 minutes. Survivors reported how Vanderbilt gave his life preserver to a woman and said to his valet, Ronald Denyer, "Save all the kiddies you can, boy." Another said Vanderbilt was "the personification of sportsmanlike coolness...the figure of a gentleman waiting for a train," as he helped women and children into lifeboats and went down with the ship.

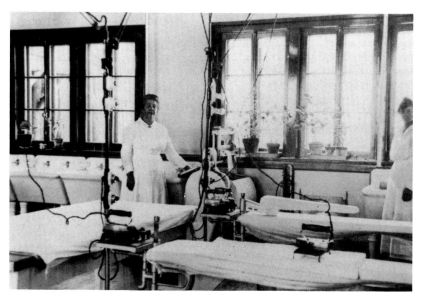

Top: *The "New Laundry," built in 1915. With its appearance unchanged, it is the "Conference Building" today.*
Bottom: *Interior of New Laundry, c. 1920. Note wash tubs, mangle, ironing boards and table for folding laundry.*

The New Laundry and Men's Camp were completed after Vanderbilt's death. The brick walls of the new stable, already four to eight feet above ground, were toppled into their foundations and covered over. When the will was probated, a trust fund of some $5 million each was established for Alfred, three, and George, one year old. Sagamore, other Adirondack properties, and $3 million were left to Vanderbilt's widow, Margaret Emerson, who was responsible for the next forty years of Sagamore's history.

The Playhouse, 1910s, with rustic fence and gates to the garden on the right.

THE WORKERS AT SAGAMORE

The history of Great Camps like Sagamore is the history of the workers who built and maintained them as much as the wealthy families who owned them. While the Vanderbilts might occupy their Adirondack camp a few weeks to two months of the year, the caretakers lived at Sagamore the year round and raised their families there. While Durant, Vanderbilt and Margaret Emerson usually are credited with the original Sagamore and its subsequent expansions, and appropriately so, it was the skilled craftsmen who executed the work and often surpassed their employer's expectations.

Schuyler Kathan was the mason who built Sagamore's original massive stone fireplaces, chimneys and foundations. He executed much of the Vanderbilts' 1901-1903 and the 1914-15 expansions as well. Charles Dougherty and James Leffler were the blacksmiths responsible for Sagamore's impressive ornamental ironwork, as well as the more mundane horseshoing and wagon maintenance that was essential to the camp's operation. Albert ("Allee") Roblee contributed much of the early carpentry, as did Garry Rogers, Josh Smith, Freeland Jones, Charlie Hunt and George Wilson. Wilson was responsible for fine rustic, twig furniture at Sagamore and was also a skilled gardener. The Frenchman Seraphin L'Etang was the craftsman probably most responsible for the many rustic beds, dressers, tables and built-in furniture still seen at Sagamore today, as well as some of the Vanderbilts' building additions.

Sagamore's first superintendent was John Callahan, who had also been superintendent at Uncas and continued with the Morgans in that capacity. When Durant began building Sagamore, Callahan hired his brother-in-law Richard Collins to work on the crew. He spent his first winter at Sagamore living in a tent while construction was underway. After Vanderbilt purchased the camp, Collins became superintendent in 1902. For the next twenty-two years, Richard and Margaret Collins remained in charge of Sagamore's operation, raising their family of five children there, deep in the Adirondack wilderness.

The Collinses were in charge of all aspects of life at Sagamore. They supervised a staff of 10-40 people, depending upon the season, whether the owners were in residence, the number of guests, and what building projects were underway. As one of their workers, Francis Pirong, recalled, "There'd be three men always working on the outside...Then there were three men in

Portraits of Sugamore workers, 1910s. The old laundry and ice house (top) and the barn (bottom) are visible behind them.

32

the barn. And then there was the blacksmith, the electrician, the painter, and the gardener and the caretaker. He didn't just sit around and count the days as they passed."

When the owners visited, they often brought their own staff with them to augment the Sagamore workers, including personal maids, chefs, butlers, valets and chauffeurs. The women staff would be enlisted, or new ones hired, to help in the kitchen, waitress, and work as laundresses, seamstresses and maids, under Margaret Collins' supervision. Aletha Shatraw, who worked briefly at Sagamore in 1923 as a maid, dusted the Main Lodge and Wigwam regularly, even when the camp was closed, just in case the owners called and announced they were coming for an unexpected stay.

For the bulk of the year when the owners were away, there was still an unremitting series of chores. The horses, cows and poultry had to be cared for and the roads kept open in all seasons. In the winter, a wooden snowplow drawn by two horses was required. Also in winter, the heavy snows were shoveled from the roofs, and ice was cut from the lake to provide year-round refrigeration in the camp's two ice houses. In the late winter and spring, maple trees were tapped and the sap boiled to make maple syrup in the sugar house, which was adjacent to the farm area across the lake. The large vegetable and flower gardens and the potato and corn fields were tilled and planted. These would provide all the vegetables for the camp the year round.

In summers, the farm, gardens and lawns were tended and the camp made ready for the owners, whose summer visit typically coincided with the racing season in Saratoga Springs. When the Vanderbilts or Mrs. Emerson were in residence, noisy or visually distracting building projects came to a halt, and the workers focused on meeting the needs of the family and guests. Staff and hired guides escorted them on hunting and fishing excursions; others set pins for the guests in the bowling alley. Others gathered large quantities of raspberries from the surrounding forests.

As autumn came, the raspberries and other produce from the garden and orchard would be canned and stored for the long winter ahead, and the pace would quicken on the continual labor of cutting, hauling, splitting and stacking firewood to fill the 100-cord woodshed that supplied the camp's original wood-burning furnaces (later converted to coal, then oil), 25 fireplaces (eventually), cookstoves and many woodstoves.

Top: *Plowing with two horse power, c. 1920. Richard Collins, Sr. is second from right*
Bottom: *Ice-cutting on a snowy day on Sagamore Lake, c. 1921.*

This was some of the normal, annual work routine. When new building construction and infrastructure improvement projects were underway, as they often were, enlarged work crews would need to be housed, fed and supervised for months at a time.

In addition to overseeing all aspects of Sagamore's operation, Richard and Margaret Collins also supervised five irrepressible children - John, Patrick, Tom, Richard and Margaret, who grew up at Sagamore. In their early years at Sagamore, the Collins family lived above the kitchen. After 1914, they lived above the New Laundry. For several years, the Collins family occupied the far wing of the second floor - Richard and Margaret Collins in one bedroom, three boys in another, their daughter Margaret in a third, and Mrs. Collins' parents, recently retired, in the fourth. Their living room was downstairs in the large room with brick fireplace and two walls of tall windows facing the lake. Their dining room was the staff dining room adjoining the kitchen. Here they entertained friends when the Vanderbilts or Mrs. Emerson were away and even threw an occasional party in the Playhouse for a wedding, sweet sixteen or other special occasion.

The Collins children attended grade school right at Sagamore. A teacher was hired to live at Sagamore during the week and teach up to eight children in the living room of the Annex in the service complex. In 1914, the Annex or "Schoolhouse" was moved, and Richard Collins, Jr. remembered actually attending school inside the building, as it inched its way down the road, pulled by a team of horses, to its present location. The four-mile road to Raquette Lake was plowed with horses and kept open year-round. Margaret Collins recalled how, in spite of the bitter cold and deep snows, she never missed a day of high school in Raquette Lake.

The Collins children participated in the work at camp, being assigned tasks appropriate to their age - picking raspberries, baking bread, "boughing down" the lean-tos or "open camps" with balsam branches, dusting, shoveling snow off the roofs, nailing bark on the buildings, and tending the horses. They also played in the woods and on the waters around Sagamore, went on family picnics and fishing trips, hiked, skied, skated on the lake, tobogganed down the huge slide erected across the lake, played the piano, used some of Sagamore's recreational facilities, and went to the annual Catholic Fair in town, the highlight of the local social season. There were also many practical jokes. In her late seventies, Margaret recalled the time her brother Tom played a joke on the guests, a time when

Top: *The Collins family, c. 1912. From left: Richard, Jr., Richard, Sr. holding Tom, Margaret, Mrs. Collins (also Margaret), Patrick and John*
Bottom: *The Collins children and friends with pet fawn, c. 1916.*

The Collins children and friends on their toboggan, c. 1916.

the papers happened to be filled with the story of a chimpanzee which had escaped from a zoo and was on the loose.

"One night just like seven o'clock, you know, when it was just getting a slight bit dusky, we were coming home here, from eating, and Tom heard some of the guests coming up from the Main Camp, and he said, 'I'm going to make believe I'm the chimpanzee...you beat it.' I said, 'Oh, don't do that, Tom. We'll get into *more* trouble.' He said, 'You beat it,' so I didn't. I wanted to be at least in sight so I could see him get slaughtered. So I went up to a little road that was there and he climbed the tree. He had glasses and there was a street light there so the light reflected on his glasses. And he waited till the people were just about under that tree and he began to shake the branches. 'It's the chimpanzee! I can see his eyes!' And I was dying up above, so I didn't know what to do, because one valet was with them and he said, 'Oh, I'll run down and get the shotgun. You wait here. I'll be right back.' So he went down, got a gun and was starting up the path and shot it just to see that it was working alright. And Tom rattled the branches and never moved. And about then my father came along and Pirong said, 'That's Tom up there.' He said, 'Tom, get down out of there.' Tom dropped right down, waiting for whatever sentence he got."

The Collins family left Sagamore in 1924 and were followed by Thomas and Millie Callahan, son of John and Mary Callahan from Camp Uncas, as superintendents. The Collins family moved to Blue Mt. Lake, where they purchased the former Duryea camp and, for many years, ran an inn there, now known as "The Hedges." The Collins children's memories are filled with both the hard work and the fun they had growing up at Sagamore. It was a unique way of life - an almost self-sufficient little community amidst the rustic elegance and natural beauty of Sagamore and the Adirondack wilderness.

THE EMERSON YEARS

With her two young sons, Margaret Emerson Vanderbilt continued to visit Sagamore, which she had come to love in the few years she had known it. Two years after the sinking of the Luisitania, tragedy almost struck the family again.

Every day the boys were taken for a carriage ride around Sagamore Lake. On one clear summer's day in 1917, when Alfred was four-and-a-half, they were out on their daily ride, Alfred in the front seat next to the driver, George and the governess seated behind them, when for no apparent reason, a large birch tree began to fall across the road above them. The driver, Johnny Hoy tried unsuccessfully to maneuver the horses and wagon back out of the way, but was killed instantly when the tree hit him. Both of Alfred's knees were broken and a large part of his scalp was dislodged. The traces connecting the horses to the wagon were broken by the falling tree, and the panicked horses galloped the rest of the way around the trail back to camp. Mrs. Vanderbilt was playing croquet on the lawn in front of the Main Lodge and young Dick Collins was in the barn when they heard the horses clattering across the bridge by Wigwam and knew something was wrong. The rescue party soon found the damaged wagon and its three traumatized occupants. Alfred recovered completely. An iron cross on the trail around Sagamore Lake still honors the memory of Johnny Hoy.

In 1918, Margaret Emerson Vanderbilt married Raymond T. Baker, the director of the United States Mint. Their daughter, Gloria Baker, was born the next year. They divorced in 1928. Within the month, Margaret married Charles M. Amory - her fourth husband. Finally, in 1934, she divorced Amory and re-assumed her maiden name.

Mrs. Emerson loved to entertain at Sagamore on a grand scale. In the summer of 1924, she drew a rough sketch in the dirt in front of the Main Lodge for her new superintendent Thomas Callahan, informing him that she wanted an addition to the dining room to be finished in time to celebrate Christmas dinner there. The new dining room, with its bay window and third and largest fireplace, was capable of comfortably seating some forty guests around its three large rustic tables. The former staff dining room was made part of an expanded kitchen, and a new, semi-detached staff dining room was constructed, adjoining the back corner of the kitchen. (A subsequent 1951 expansion joined the main dining

Top: *Mrs. Emerson (front row, center) and guests on steps of Main Lodge, late 1930s. Gloria Baker is seated to her right.*
Bottom: *Mrs. Emerson's bedroom, second floor, Main Lodge.*

room to Durant's original dining room, increased the capacity further and, in a different configuration, seats 100 guests today.)

In the early twenties, the old laundry was expanded to serve as Gloria's nursery, and in 1925, when Alfred and George were approaching their teenage years, the "Cabins" (Lakeside Cottage) was expanded to its present size. As they became young adults, this was the "bachelor's quarters," where Alfred, George and their friends stayed when they visited Sagamore. After George married in 1935, Gloria's former nursery became "George's Cottage." When Alfred married in 1937, a new, little cottage was constructed for him along the lake shore. When Gloria married a year later, a slightly larger version of Alfred's cottage was constructed for her, the last new building to be built at Sagamore.

In her heyday, in the 1920s and 30s, Mrs. Emerson was considered one of the best loved of all the great social hostesses. (She shared much in common with Marjorie Merriweather Post, who entertained with equal lavishness at her Camp Topridge in the northern Adirondacks.) Sagamore was referred to in the newspapers as "the playground of the millionaires" and headquarters of "the gaming crowd." Mrs. Emerson once said, "I like every game there is. We must have played fifty of them a day [at Sagamore] and more at night." She herself was an excellent croquet player and often enjoyed besting her guests at this game. A typical day of on-going competitions at Sagamore is well illustrated by the poem one wag inserted into the lodge guest book during the summer of 1937:

> At the crack o' noon at Sagamore
> The battle's on for blood and gore,
> For everythin's a contest there,
> And while you test the bill-of-fare
> Somebody says, "Guess who I am."
> (Though nobody may give a damn.)
> You venture, "Are you someone dead?"
> Or maybe, "You're a mare who's bred."
> Perhaps you are a kind of fly
> (The kind you do trout fishing by.)
> When dinner's over rest your soul
> But not your carcass - you must bowl.
> Or play at ping or pong or pool,
> For Sport is King and Kings must rule.
> And so to bed at Sagamore
> To listen to young Alfred snore.

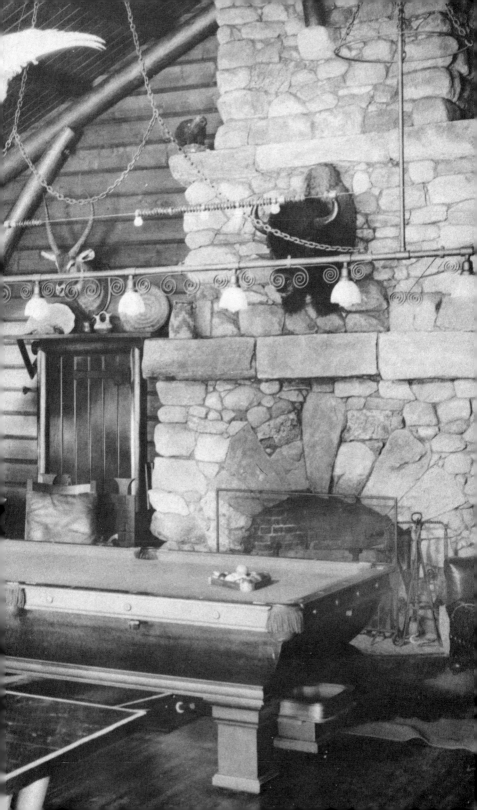

Gerald Baltz remembered how Alfred's seaplane always scared the roosters and hens, as it flew over the service complex, landing on the lake after returning from a day at the races in Saratoga Springs. (Baltz worked at Sagamore and was the son of Bertha and Joe Lamb, who followed the Callahans as superintendents in the late 30s and 40s.)

Mrs. Emerson surrounded herself with the most prominent figures in politics, finance, entertainment and high society, such as actor and actresses Gary Cooper, Gene Tierney and Jean Arthur, musicians Eddy Duchin and Hoagey Carmichael, heavyweight champion Gene Tunney, socialites Lord Mountbatten and Bobo Rockefeller, and financier Bernard Baruch. After J.P. Morgan died, she purchased Camp Uncas in 1947 and leased it for a period to General George Marshall, the Secretary of State, who entertained Madame Chiang Kai-Shek there in 1949. They, too, were Margaret Emerson's guests at Sagamore. The visits of these notables to the Adirondack camp were often the topic of the society gossip columns of the day. Mrs. Emerson even erected an expensive gravestone for her friend's dog, "Inky," who was buried at Sagamore.

Sagamore remained a center of the "gaming crowd" until the outbreak of World War II, when Mrs. Emerson served in the Pacific theater of action as assistant to the commissioner of the American Red Cross. Dorothy Rogers, wife of Richard Rogers of Rogers and Hammerstein fame, was a good friend of Margaret Emerson and, in her memoirs, recalled the contrast of life at Sagamore in the pre-war and the war years. Before the war, it was customary for the women guests to be served breakfast in bed. During the war, in keeping with the national austerity program, the women came to breakfast in the dining room. "It was rough," quipped Mrs. Rogers.

After the war, as philanthropic activities occupied more of her time, and her health began to fail, Mrs. Emerson began to use Sagamore less often. In 1953-55, in a series of three transactions, she donated Sagamore to Syracuse University for use in their education programs.

Overleaf: *The Playhouse ("Casino"), 1915-1924.*

SYRACUSE UNIVERSITY

Syracuse University already owned two other conference centers which had been donated to them in the Adirondacks - Camp Pinebrook on Upper Saranac Lake and Camp Minnowbrook on Blue Mt. Lake. Thus, Syracuse was a natural choice when Mrs. Emerson decided it was time to divest herself of the camp she had loved for almost half a century.

For the first decade, Syracuse used Sagamore in the summer as a children's reading camp. Thousands of college-bound high school students spent several weeks at Sagamore, improving their reading and study skills and enjoying the outdoor activities of a typical Adirondack children's summer camp, not to mention the Playhouse, bowling alleys and ambiance of the former Vanderbilt family estate.

In the spring and fall, and then also in summer from the mid-sixties to mid-seventies, Syracuse used Sagamore for adult education programs and conferences. As the university described it, "Adults from education, government, business, industry, and the professions participate in programs especially developed for them by the university. Conferences vary in size from twenty to one hundred people, in duration from one weekend to six weeks, and in subject matter from technical areas of research and engineering to the arts and liberal education."

The entertainment center that Vanderbilt and Mrs. Emerson had created at Durant's Adirondack camp converted relatively easily into a college conference center. The Dining Room and the New Laundry (renamed the Conference Building) each seated some 100 people for meals and meetings. Smaller meeting rooms were available in the New Laundry's former living room, and the lounges of the Main Lodge, Wigwam and Lakeside Cottages. The Playhouse and Bowling Alley fulfilled their original purposes, and bedrooms in the Main Lodge (7), Wigwam (9), the Conference Building (11), Lakeside (6), Alfred's Cottage (2), Gloria's Cottage (2), George's Cottage (2), and the Men's Camp (9) provided ample sleeping accommodations for over 100 guests.

During this entire period, the maintenance of and housekeeping for Sagamore were placed in the hands of Bruce and Mary Darling. The Darlings lived in the first floor of the Men's Camp, where they raised their own family. Assisted by a considerably smaller staff than ever before at Sagamore, they did an excellent job of maintaining the camp's interiors, in spite of the

Top: *Reading instruction in the Conference Building, c. 1960.*
Bottom: *Relaxing after hours in the Wigwam lounge, c. 1960.*

hardest use the buildings had ever seen. Syracuse University had less of a commitment to the exteriors. Some of the farm buildings across the lake were dismantled or decayed in the late fifties and sixties, and several of the buildings in the caretaking complex were removed. For the last seven years of Syracuse's ownership, the main camp's exteriors were put on a deferred maintenance plan.

In the mid-1970s, many private colleges around the United States were beginning to run into financial difficulties, and Syracuse was no exception. It had sold its Camp Pinebrook some years earlier and now concluded that too much of its assets were still tied up in Adirondack real estate. Quietly Sagamore was put on the market.

The State of New York, eager to add Sagamore's 1526 acres to the State Forest Preserve, contracted to purchase the entire property for $650,000. But just before the closing, historic preservationists across New York State realized that, if the State did take title to Sagamore, the buildings would have to be destroyed. Article 14 of the state constitution, passed in the last century, before Sagamore and most of the Great Camps had even been built, said that all land the state owned within the Adirondack Forest Preserve must remain "forever wild" and could not be sold, leased or traded. In the past, when the state acquired land with buildings, they always razed the buildings or allowed them to rot.

To avoid this fate for Sagamore, the newly formed Preservation League of New York State worked out with the state and Syracuse University an unprecedented arrangement. On October 1, 1975, the state would take title to 1517 acres of mostly vacant land around Sagamore, including the entire lake, for which it would pay the university $550,000. Then the state would have thirty days in which to find a *third party* to purchase the main buildings, on about eight acres, for the remaining $100,000 of the purchase price.

In return for this exceptionally low price, the new owner would have to agree to: maintain Sagamore in good condition or else the state could repossess the property without compensation; make no major architectural changes; let Syracuse use the property one more year; serve no alcoholic beverages on the property; use no motorboats on the lake; make the property available one day a week in the summer for public viewing, and other restrictions that would be passed on with Sagamore's deed, including the provision that, if the property were ever resold, it must be sold for only $100,000 plus the value of subsequent improvements. There was a serious question as to whether an owner could be found on so short notice who would be willing to take on the responsibility for Sagamore with such restrictive conditions.

Meanwhile, in the northern Adirondacks, near Lake Placid, the National Humanistic Education Center, a non-profit, educational organization, had operated a conference center in the village of Upper Jay for the previous five years. Based at its 178-acre converted farm site, the organization specialized in teacher training, human relations training, and outdoor and environmental education. For years, its directors, Howard Kirschenbaum and Barbara Glaser, had been combing the Adirondacks for a more suitable conference site. They heard of Sagamore's availability on October 9. Fourteen days later the Education Center was selected from among the bidders, and nine days thereafter, on November 1, 1975, on schedule, the closing took place in Sagamore's Main Lodge. The unencumbered title first passed to the Preservation League of New York State. Immediately, the Preservation League resold the property to the Education Center with a deed containing all the preservation covenants and restrictions that had been agreed upon previously.

Thus the Preservation League of New York State helped save an historic site from destruction, Syracuse University received its full sales price, the state of New York got what it called "a compatible neighbor" to the State Forest Preserve, and the Education Center - later renamed Sagamore Institute in honor of the new site - found its ideal conference center.

Shortly after the purchase, Sagamore was listed on the National. Register of Historic Places. Before the new owners took possession, Syracuse University sold Sagamore's contents at auction. Fortunately, before and during the auction, Sagamore's directors were able to purchase about 80% of the original furnishings which Syracuse had owned.

The New York Times

State Buys Vanderbilts' Adirondack Camp

TUESDAY, OCTOBER 7, 1975

New York State has just purchased Sagamore, the 1,500-acre Adirondack Mountain Camp that was used by the Vanderbilts in the early ninteen hundreds, to add to the "forever wild" section of the Adirondack Forest Preserve.

But the acquisition has created a major problem that is causing great concern among architects, state officials and others interested in historic preservation—how to prevent the demolition of the elaborate rustic buildings that are the foremost examples of Adirondack - camp architecture, a combination of simple log construction with ornate Swiss chalet decorations.

Through an irony of protectionism, the buildings would have to be torn down if they were on land purchased by the state, according to the prevailing interpretation by state officials of Article 14 of the State Constitution, which mandates keeping the Adirondack area "forever wild."

No one seriously believes that the buildings of Sagamore will actually be torn down immediately, but the State lacks funds to maintain them, and thus they could deteriorate until they

Continued on Page 45, Column 1

SUNDAY, NOVEMBER 9, 1975

VANDERBILT CAMP BOUGHT FOR STATE

Sagamore Lake Buildings to Be Used by Public

By HAROLD FABER

The luxurious camp buildings of the Vanderbilts' on Sagamore Lake in the Adirondacks have been purchased by a nonprofit organization and will be preserved for use by the public, the state's Department of Environmental Conservation has announced.

Last month, the state bought the 1,518-acre estate for $550,000 to add to the Adirondack Park Preserve, but a seven-acre island and its buildings were excluded from the sale because of a problem in preventing their demolition.

According to the prevailing interpretation by state officials of Article 14 of the State Constitution, the "forever wild" clause, they are required to tear down any buildings on land purchased by the state in the preserve.

Bought for $100,000

On Nov. 1 at Sagamore,

49

SAGAMORE INSTITUTE

With a workshop led by Carl R. Rogers, the internationally renowned psychologist and educator, Sagamore Institute commenced its first season of operation in the summer of 1977. Since then, its residential programs have continued to expand in number and scope and have been attended by over twenty thousand people from across the country and many nations. Beginning in 1980, when Sagamore was further winterized to house visitors to the Winter Olympic Games in Lake Placid, the Institute has offered weekend and weeklong programs throughout the year.

Adirondack history, architecture and crafts constitute a central focus of Sagamore's program. The crisis over Sagamore's fate in 1975 suddenly alerted the public to the special value of the thirty to forty "Adirondack Great Camps" and the much broader regional architectural style they represent. This awareness coincided with a revival of interest in Adirondack regional arts and crafts. Sagamore Institute quickly became a leading organization for interpreting and advocating the preservation of the Adirondack Great Camps and for conducting tours of some of the major camps throughout the year. Workshops on traditional Adirondack arts and crafts include rustic furniture, Adirondack basketry, snowshoes, storytelling, woodcarving, painting and illustrating nature, and mountain music and dance. Adirondack railroads, steamboats, and other subjects are the focus of weekend programs on Adirondack history.

Outdoor recreation and environmental education are a second major thrust of Sagamore Institute's programming. Winter ski weekends, summer recreation weekends, hiking, fishing, mountain climbing, llama trekking, canoe trips, and women's outdoor programs are offered for all ages and abilities. Attempting to address the critical environmental issues of the day, Sagamore also offers programs on environmental topics, nature awareness, and personal and professional development programs for environmental activists.

Professional training and personal growth programs have also remained a significant part of Sagamore's curriculum. Management training, new methods in teaching, preparing organizations for the integration of a diverse workforce, burn-out prevention for professionals, women and leadership, using humor and creativity in the workplace, counseling skills, and improving personal relationships are a sample of the professional and personal growth workshops regularly scheduled at Sagamore.

Top: *A seminar meeting outdoors.*
Bottom: *Returning to Sagamore after ski touring through the surrounding Forest Preserve.*

Top: *A school class learning history, science and other subjects in a unique setting.*
Bottom: *A work weekend at Sagamore. Some volunteers paint the trim on Alfred's Cottage, while others install a drain pipe.*

Family and youth programs round out Sagamore's residential schedule. A grandparents and grandchildren's summer camp, family weekend, youth and teen wilderness programs, and personal growth workshop for teens have been typical summer themes.

In the spaces between Sagamore's scheduled programs, other organizations and groups use the facility for their meetings and programs. The national Elderhostel organization and area colleges, for example, often bring groups to Sagamore. Almost all of Sagamore Institute's income is derived from programs such as these. Lacking the financial depth of Alfred Vanderbilt, Margaret Emerson or Syracuse University, the Institute instead has relied on the good will and energies of the thousands of people who have participated in its programs. A member's organization has provided the funds to purchase materials for preservation and restoration of the buildings. Hundreds of volunteers, skilled and unskilled, supervised by Sagamore's director and superintendent, following a preservation plan developed by professional architects, have contributed many thousands of hours of labor.

Since 1977, for example, the Memorial Day Work Weekend has attracted some seventy volunteers to work on all aspects of Sagamore's maintenance and restoration - landscaping, road work, painting, carpentry repairs, window washing, oiling all the interior wood surfaces, roofing, and the like. Certified electricians, plumbers, sheet metal workers, engineers, archaeologists, architects, landscapers and other skilled craftspeople have similarly given freely of their time and talents throughout the year. Beginning in the late 1980s, special grants from the New York State Council on the Arts and several foundations and corporations have also helped enhance the restoration program.

With all this assistance, Sagamore's buildings and grounds have improved steadily since its transfer from Syracuse University. A new sewage treatment system, emergency generator, and massive new electric work, including restoring the original outdoor lighting fixtures, have dramatically improved Sagamore's infrastructure. New roofs, porches, rotted log replacements, painting, landscaping and other improvements have similarly enhanced the camp's long-term preservation and attractiveness. The interiors have continued to be maintained in excellent condition.

Top: *Grandparents and grandchildren's summer camp at Sagamore. The author's parents and daughter are in the second row.* Bottom: *The class photo. A group of educators ending a summer workshop.*

54

THE LAND EXCHANGE

In the late 1970s and early 1980s, the Adirondack Great Camps and Sagamore in particular attracted increasing attention among history and architecture buffs and the general public. Craig Gilborn's book on the Durant family (see Acknowledgements), Harvey Kaiser's book on *The Great Camps of the Adirondacks* (Boston: David Godine, 1982), many national magazine articles on the Great Camps, and Sagamore's own programs led to Sagamore's existence and significance becoming known to an increasing number of people. All this attention, however, paled before the publicity that Sagamore received in 1983 - the culmination of many years of behind-the-scenes work to save the Sagamore caretaking complex.

Back in 1975, in the last-minute rush to save Sagamore from destruction, the State of New York drew the boundary line so narrowly around the main buildings that they excluded the eleven adjoining buildings of the camp's caretaking or service complex. This was consistent with state policy to eliminate or at least limit the private inholdings within the Forest Preserve, and they further reasoned that any new owners of Sagamore would have their hands filled just maintaining the main buildings. The state assumed that a new owner would be relieved not to have the added responsibility of taking care of the eleven caretaking buildings which were in much worse repair and appeared to have little architectural significance.

Unfortunately, this logic left out two considerations, one which might have been obvious, one which was more subtle. First, on a practical level, the new owner of Sagamore would be hard-pressed to get along without the storage, workshop and additional staff housing space the caretaking complex provided. Of equal significance, beginning with the 1975 crisis over Sagamore's fate, professional and public attention first focused on the phenomenon of the Adirondack Great Camp. Architectural historians began pointing out how unique these great rustic estates were as little, self-sufficient villages in the wilderness, with their own architectural plan, fabric, artistry and decor, and their own way of life for generations of families who owned, lived and worked at them. More and more it became apparent that to have half a Great Camp was not to have a Great Camp at all. Without the worker's complex, Sagamore's special role as a prototypic Adirondack Great Camp could not be appreciated. Moreover, to save the buildings associated with the rich and famous owners while allowing the workers' heritage to be destroyed would be to perpetuate an outmoded concept of social history.

Sagamore was not the only Great Camp in danger. Camps Santanoni, Topridge and Nehasene had also come into state ownership by various means and were similarly threatened with destruction. Recognizing a possible generic conflict between the goals of environmental conservation and historic preservation, New York's Lt. Governor Marianne Krupsak convened a high-level conference at Camp Topridge on "Cultural Heritage in the Wilds." This led to several committees assigned to propose solutions for the four camps already in state ownership and the longer-term problem they represented. After two years of periodic deliberations, it became clear that the committees were failing to achieve any consensus on recommendations to solve the problem. Meanwhile, the state was soliciting bids to begin dismantling some of the caretaking buildings at Sagamore.

Sagamore's executive director Howard Kirschenbaum finally concluded that, if the caretaking buildings were going to be saved, Sagamore would have to come up with a plan and initiate the process itself. He drafted an amendment to Article 14 of the state constitution that would provide an exception from the "forever wild" provision specifically to save the eleven service buildings at Sagamore. The concept was simple. Sagamore Institute would purchase approximately 200 acres of forest land elsewhere in the Adirondacks and would trade this land to the state in exchange for the caretaking complex at Sagamore on about ten acres. Thus, at no cost to the taxpayers, the Forest Preserve would be enhanced by almost 200 acres and the entire Camp Sagamore would be reunited.

To oversimplify a long and difficult struggle, with the help and leadership of the Preservation League of New York State, working in tandem with Sagamore, the legislation was introduced in 1982 and passed the legislature that spring, with an almost unanimous vote. After the new legislature was elected that fall, the bill was passed again by both houses, almost unanimously, in the spring of 1983. To amend the state constitution, however, not only is the approval of two sessions of the state legislature required, the voters of New York State must also approve the change by a public referendum. There were now six months before the November election to convince millions of New York State voters, most of whom had never heard of Sagamore, of the wisdom of changing the state constitution to protect a few, plain old buildings in the Adirondack Mountains. Rather, they needed to be persuaded that

SAVE SAGAMORE

VOTE YES
November 8
Ballot Proposal 6

Your vote will help
- Reunite and preserve Camp Sagamore, listed on the National Register of Historic Places, for future generations
- Save 11 historic buildings from decay or destruction
- Add 200 acres of wild forest land to the Adirondack Forest Preserve
- Do all this at no cost to New York State taxpayers

This ballot proposal is supported by the following organizations:

Adirondack Conservation Council•Adirondack Council•Adirondack Museum of the Adirondack Historical Association•Adirondack Mountain Club•Adirondack North Country Association•Association for the Protection of the Adirondacks•Chautauqua Institution•Environmental Planning Lobby•Landmark Society of Western New York•Municipal Art Society of New York•National Audubon Society•National Trust for Historic Preservation•Natural Resources Defense Council•New York Landmarks Conservancy•New York State Association of Architects/AIA•New York State Board for Historic Preservation•N.Y.S. Department of Environmental Conservation•N.Y.S. Office of Parks, Recreation and Historic Preservation•Preservation League of New York State•Regional Conference of Historical Agencies•Saranac Lake Chamber of Commerce•Sagamore Institute•Scenic Hudson, Inc.•Society for the Preservation of Long Island Antiquities•and many others.

Co-Chairmen, Coalition to Save Camp Sagamore

Senator Alfonse D'Amato   Brendan Gill
Senator Daniel Patrick Moynihan   Mrs. James Houghton

For more information, contact:
Preservation League of New York State
307 Hamilton Street
Albany, N.Y. 12210
518-462-5658

Preservation League of New York State

destroying these buildings, which represented a way of life to generations of Adirondack families, would be an irreparable loss of an important part of the Adirondacks' and the state's cultural heritage.

Again the Preservation League proved an invaluable ally, as they organized the statewide "Coalition to Save Camp Sagamore" to educate the voters on the issues involved. U.S. Senators Moynihan and D'Amato agreed to serve as honorary co-chairmen of the Coalition. With press conferences, tours, bumper stickers, lapel buttons, flyers, editorials, speeches and a booth at the State Fair, the Preservation League and Sagamore Institute took the campaign to every corner of the state. When the voters went to the polls on November 8, 62% of them - over 1,550,000 people - voted to approve the land exchange in a landslide victory, with the Sagamore amendment faring better than any of the eight propositions on the statewide ballot that year.

Part of the caretaking complex, 1930s The electrician's house, known as "Ryan's Cottage" (removed c. 1960), is on the right.

A LIVING GREAT CAMP

The legal work which took nine days to accomplish when Sagamore's main complex was saved in 1975 took three years for the caretaking complex after the 1983 referendum. Eventually, however, the eleven buildings were transferred to Sagamore Institute's ownership, creating an eighteen acre compound with some twenty-eight buildings, all protected for future generations by a uniform set of covenants and restrictions built into a forty-page deed to the entire property.

Since then, Sagamore Institute has rehabilitated most of the caretaking complex, giving new life to many buildings which were essentially abandoned or not maintained for ten to thirty years. Not only have the buildings been preserved, but many have been returned to their original uses. The carpenter's shop is now being used to build rustic furniture, much as when Allee Roblee, George Wilson and Seraphin L'Etang built Sagamore's rustic furniture almost a hundred years ago. The fire in the blacksmith's forge has been rekindled, as visiting blacksmiths repair the ornamental iron work first made there and create new work in the Sagamore tradition. In the future, Sagamore plans to use the other workshop areas to demonstrate and produce the rustic crafts associated with the region - Adirondack guide-boats, Adirondack pack baskets, balsam pillows, snowshoes, and more.

Although, by deed, Sagamore Institute is required to allow public viewing only one day per week in the summer season, and has done at least that since 1976, Sagamore expanded its public viewing schedule in the late 1980s to six days a week during the summer and weekends in the early fall. Thousands of visitors each year now drive down the four-mile dirt road south of Raquette Lake to visit Sagamore, tour many of the buildings, see the crafts and craftshops, and experience Sagamore's historical and present-day ambiance.

Unlike a house museum, however, to which visitors come briefly, look, do not touch, and leave, Sagamore has evolved again into a "living Great Camp." People sleep in its rustic and contemporary beds. The dining room is alive with the sound of talking and eating around the large communal tables. Wood smoke comes from the many chimneys, and boaters and canoeists paddle on Sagamore Lake. Craftsmen produce classic Adirondack crafts in the workshops and perpetuate the tradition by teaching the crafts to others. Caretakers and staff occupy buildings the year round, and their children are raised there and attend school in

Top: *Blacksmith John Breed instructing an apprentice.*
Bottom: *Stitching the annual "Sagamore Quilt."*

Raquette Lake. As much as Sagamore changes, it remains the same - a century after it was built.

Beyond most visitors' fascination with Sagamore's extraordinary scale, style, design and setting, is perhaps an unconscious awareness of how Sagamore embodies a classic American paradox. Particularly since this country's Gilded Age, Americans have been fascinated with the lifestyles of the rich and famous. The glitter of Hollywood and all it symbolizes has been a Siren-song, appealing to almost universal fantasies of wealth, fame, beauty of a sort, and power. At the same time, true to their frontier heritage, Americans have been ready to return to nature. Since Thoreau and the New England Transcendentalists, the simplicity, naturalness and basic truths of living in harmony with nature have been an important and ongoing part of the American soul and psyche. At Sagamore, both of these often competing and contradictory sets of values are dramatically represented.

Ironically, William West Durant's efforts of the past century have been far more significant than he could ever have imagined. Built as a luxury camp for the wealthy, Sagamore has become the most accessible of all the Adirondack Great Camps. Designed in the romantic images of James Fenimore Cooper, the Tyrolean Alps and the log cabin, Sagamore has perhaps greater meaning for our age than it did for Durant's. In at least three of its qualities, Sagamore speaks clearly to the present, as much as it reflects the past.

First, Sagamore was built to last. As our society begins to appreciate the importance of conserving and recycling its natural resources, Sagamore stands as a symbol of durability, of building for the future. Its solid masonry and wood and log construction are the very antithesis of a throw-away society. Sagamore puts us in touch with our past and inspires us to conserve that which we hold dear - the beauty of our natural environment and the best of our human creations. By evoking our sense of history, Sagamore causes us to reflect on our values for the future and calls upon us to create a world as lovely and durable as that which we find on the shore of Sagamore Lake.

Second, Sagamore was built with natural materials. As society painfully comes to understand the dangers of chemical pollution and nuclear wastes in the environment, it is heartening to realize that perhaps 98% of Sagamore is made of stone and wood. When Sagamore eventually does return to the soil, nature will be none the worse for it. Although it is unrealistic to expect cities to be built exclusively of stone and wood, it is useful to be reminded of the versatility, durability and creativity possible with natural materials. Sagamore reminds its visitors of this important option.

Finally, Sagamore was built in harmony with nature. Many architects have commented on Durant's talent for blending his buildings into the surrounding environment. Even a building as large as the three-story Main Lodge does not appear overbearing. Sagamore demonstrates that we can achieve beauty and elegance and, at the same time, enhance our appreciation of nature. As the Adirondack Park and the planet determine their future in the 21st century and beyond, Sagamore stands as a symbol of William West Durant's design philosophy - to not only survive in nature, but to do so with style, balancing human interests with the natural world.

Sagamore's centennial in 1997 is only the beginning of its story. With continued care from its owners and friends, it will remain for centuries for future generations to enjoy. And the learnings and values people experience at Sagamore will continue to be carried back to and make a difference in the world outside.

Sagamore Lake and the Blue Ridge Wilderness - as it appeared to William West Durant...as it appears today.

"SAGAMORE"

by Dan Berggren

We all need a place every now and then
Where we can get away
To a favorite spot,
Or a state of mind,
And I found the place today.

(Chorus)
Sagamore, a bit of history,
Sagamore, and now it's part of me.
A home in the woods, a place on the shore,
Going back to Sagamore.

We all need some time every once in a while
When we can get away,
To sort out our thoughts,
To listen and to learn,
And I found the time today. (Chorus)

We all need some friends every now and then,
To help us find our way,
A shoulder to cry on,
A pat on the back,
And I found some friends today. (Chorus)

MAP OF SAGAMORE TODAY

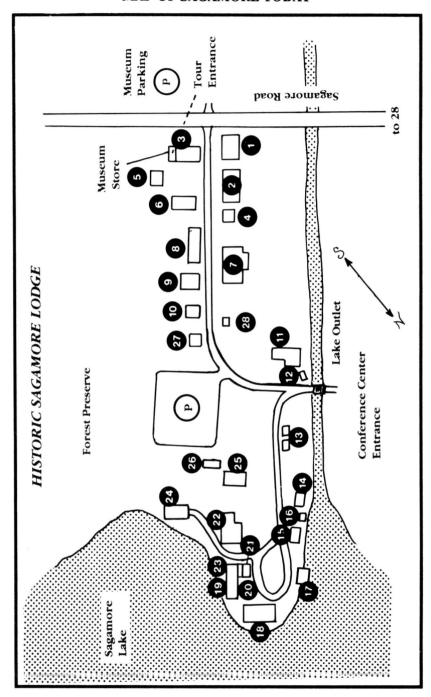

SUMMARY OF BUILDINGS TODAY

1. Carpenter's Shop, c. 1914. The carpentry and paint shop was used for woodworking and painting at Sagamore. It presently serves as a shop for making rustic furniture.

2. Woodshed, c. 1898. This original Durant woodshed held 100 cords for Sagamore's many needs, including 25 fireplaces. It is presently used for wood storage and displays. The small frame tool shed or coal bin on the west end of the woodshed was completed between 1899 and 1911.

3. Chalet (Men's Camp), 1915. Built as living quarters for workers. From 1955-76 the Darling family lived on the first floor as caretakers for Syracuse University. A 1940s addition now serves as Sagamore's store and tour entrance, offices and staff housing.

4. Small Building (Dwelling), c. 1914. The use of this building is unknown and it was possibly moved to its present location. It may have served as temporary living quarters for extra workers during the 1914-15 construction period.

5. Ice House, c. 1920. This ice house served the caretaking complex at a time when the Men's Camp, Annex (School House) and Ryan's Cottage (no longer standing) were all occupied by caretaking staff and families.

6. Hen House, 1899, c. 1914. A hen house stood across the road from the wood shed in 1899. A larger hen house was located behind the new Men's Camp in 1914 and probably was moved to its present location in 1916. Parts of the current building may date to 1899. At all three locations the hen house had large, fenced-in poultry yards.

7. Barn, c. 1898. The original barn, still standing, contained stables for work and riding horses, tack room, teamsters' room, apartment and hayloft upstairs, and a cow shed on the west end, with an adjoining yard. The Vanderbilts, who sometimes brought their own riding horses with them when visiting Sagamore, had an addition built on the east end and a section for washing wagons in the back, between 1901-1910. Later, a concrete floor was poured, including a pit, for automobile storage and maintenance.

8. Carriage House, c. 1898. The four bays on the left comprised the original Durant carriage house. The new wing on the right with three additional bays and floor was built between 1901-1910. Fancy carriages were kept on the left side and everyday carriages on the right.

9. School House (Annex), 1901-1910. Originally a building for staff housing, it was also used early in the century as a school for the caretakers' children from Sagamore and the neighboring camps. It was moved to its present site in 1914 and later used as housing for Alfred and George Vanderbilt's chauffeurs, Max and Andrew Timmons.

10. Blacksmith Shop, c. 1898. Much of the ornamental hardware around Sagamore was fashioned in this shop. It served for shoeing horses, repairing wagons, etc. The shop has been restored to its original function, blacksmithing.

11. Wigwam, c. 1901, 1914. Wigwam was built and expanded as a guest cottage for the Vanderbilts. Its bark siding suggests the name "Wigwam," an Algonquin word describing a bark covered dwelling.

12. Lean-to, after 1916. This lean-to was reconstructed in 1978 from the original one on this site and a second one near Lakeside Cottage. This example is a more polished version of the original Adirondack "open camp," used by early guides and visitors to the region.

13. Powerhouse, c. 1930. Originally housed a diesel generator for use in emergencies when the newly installed commercial electricity went out. It still provides that same function today. The adjacent shed may be the original Garden Shed, moved from the crest of the hill by the parking area.

14. Gloria's Cottage, 1939. The most recent building at Sagamore, built for Gloria Baker, Margaret Emerson's daughter from her third marriage to Raymond Baker.

15. Alfred's Cottage, 1937. Built for Alfred G. Vanderbilt II, after his marriage, this two-room cottage followed the same concept as George's and later Gloria's Cottages. The separate cabin with a bedroom and sitting room was intended to give the older children a sense of independence and privacy when, as adults with spouses, they visited Sagamore.

16. Pump House, 1914. Built when the Vanderbilts installed a modern water and sewage system at Sagamore.

17. Boat Shed, c. 1898. This original Durant structure shows a "Japanesque" influence and was used to store the several Adirondack guideboats always present at Sagamore.

18. Main Lodge, 1897. With spruce slabs nailed on the frame structure to give a log building appearance, the Lodge is the culmination of Durant's many camp designs. Four stages of railing design may be observed in the Main Lodge porches.

19. Dining Room, c. 1898, 1901 and 1924. The dining room was built in stages. Alfred Vanderbilt doubled Durant's original length and added a second fireplace; Margaret Emerson added the bay window and a third fireplace in 1924, to accommodate her many dinner guests.

20. Covered Walkway, c. 1899. A typical Adirondack Great Camp feature, the covered walkway sheltered workers moving between buildings.

21. George's Cottage (Old Laundry), c. 1898, c. 1920, c. 1935. The right half of the building is original and was used as the laundry for the early camp. Later expanded for Gloria's nursery, it was probably renovated again in 1935, when it became George Vanderbilt's cottage.

22. Conference Building (New Laundry), 1915. The New Laundry provided work and living space for the Vanderbilts' increasingly large staff. As in the past, it presently serves as Sagamore's administrative offices and provides guest accommodations and a library/meeting room.

23. Ice House, c. 1898. An original Durant building, this ice house served the main complex at Sagamore, with ice cut from the lake in winter.

24. Lakeside Cottage, c. 1901, 1925. Built by Vanderbilt as "The Incubator" or Nursery. It was later called "The Cabins," expanded and used as "bachelor's quarters" by Alfred and George until their own cottages were built. Named "Lakeside" by Syracuse University, it presently houses Sagamore staff.

25. Meeting Room (Playhouse, Casino), 1901. Designed by architect William Coulter. Furnished with billiards table, Ping-pong table, games, and various animal trophies from around the world.

26. Bowling Alley, 1914. This alley built by Alfred Vanderbilt has withstood warping and buckling for over three-quarters of a century and is still used today. With a large stone fireplace and heavy canvas curtains, the alley is semi-outdoor.

27. Root Cellar, c. 1899. The present parking lot and lawn area was once a large flower and vegetable garden, and the cellar was used to store root vegetables from the garden. An 1899 photograph taken by Seneca Ray Stoddard shows the root cellar with its original pitched roof.

28. Valve House (Privy), date unknown. Found rotting in the woods, repaired and moved to this location in 1987, this little building may have been an outhouse for Durant or Vanderbilt's staff. It presently covers two manholes for the reservoir water system.

AFTERWORD

The Board and staff of Sagamore gratefully acknowledge Howard Kirschenbaum's contributions to the founding of Sagamore Institute. We also offer a debt of thanks for his vision and strength of purpose in the unification and preservation of Great Camp Sagamore.

While Sagamore's historic structures will continue to be lovingly preserved, it is the programmatic aspects of our calendar which put the life and spirit inside the walls of our Great Camp. It is Sagamore's mission to increasingly celebrate Adirondack culture, craft, and ecology by offering programs which link grandparents, grandchildren, teens, youths, women and men with nature.

The Gilded Age believed in manifest destiny, but as we approach the 21st century, we realize that it is only through cooperation and appreciation of the natural world that we can continue a meaningful lifestyle. Issues need to be explored and Sagamore affords the perfect place for reflection and involvement.

Sagamore has been recognized by Durant, the Vanderbilts, Syracuse University and Sagamore Institute as a place apart. Dr. Howard Kirschenbaum is part of the continuum which has realized the potential of the Sagamore complex and was instrumental in preserving its character at a crucial hour. We thank Howie for his hard work, his perseverance, and his legacy of preservation which has been given to us.

Beverly Bridger
Executive Director

Left: *Furniture maker Jackson Levi Smith working on a rustic, mosaic twig design in the carpenter's shop.*

69

PHOTO CREDITS

Cover	Sagamore Institute
4	Ed Hohenstein
5	Howard Kirschenbaum
8	Margaret Collins Cunningham
10	Record & Epler/Adirondack Museum
12	Neill Kramer
17	Herbert Birrell
19	Sagamore Institute
	Helen Collins
22	Seneca Ray Stoddard/M.C. Cunningham
24	Sagamore Institute
27	Gerald Baltz
	Margaret Collins Cunningham
29	Sagamore Institute
	Margaret Collins Cunningham
30	Margaret Collins Cunningham
32	Sophia Roffe
	Sophia Roffe & M.C. Cunningham
34	Margaret Collins Cunningham
	Francis Pirong & M.C. Cunningham
36	Margaret Collins Cunningham
	Helen Collins
37	Margaret Collins Cunningham
40	Gerald Baltz
	Margaret Collins Cunningham
42-43	Margaret Collins Cunningham
46	Sagamore Institute
	Sagamore Institute
49	New York Times
51	Howard Kirschenbaum
	Bill Pearson
52	Susan Schafstall
	Joe Pfeiffer
54	Arthur & Carol Kornhaber
	Sagamore Institute
57	Mark Peckham & Preservation League of NYS
58	Bruce Darling
60	Sue Menke
	Jane Waddington
62	Virginia Conard
64	Kathy Keefer
68	Charlotte Kimball

ACKNOWLEDGMENTS

To Harold K. Hochschild, whose *Township 34* (Adirondack Museum reprints, 1952) revealed the importance of the Durant family, the development of the Durant camps, and the role of the workers in Adirondack cultural history.

To Craig Gilborn, whose book *Durant: The Fortunes and Woodland Camps of a Family in the Adirondacks* (Blue Mt. Lake: Adirondack Museum, 1981) remains the definitive work on the Durant family.

To the Adirondack Museum, whose galleries, archives, library and photograph collection have been an invaluable source of information over the years, and to its staff, who have always been most generous with their help and support.

To Howard Lewis Applegate, who prepared the first short monograph on Sagamore's history.

To Paul Malo, whose early interpretations on the significance of the Adirondack Great Camps educated us all.

To Jeannine Laverty, Carl Stearns, Neill Kramer and Kathy Keefer for their research and contributions to Sagamore's history.

To Karen Lux for her extensive oral histories of Sagamore's former workers and their families.

To Margaret Collins Cunningham, Richard Collins, Jr., Francis Pirong, Gerald and Marianne Baltz, Anthony Garvan, and the many other individuals who shared so freely their memories, photographs and memorabilia of life and work at Sagamore and the nearby Great Camps.

To Beverly Bridger, Executive Director, and to the Sagamore staff for their support and assistance on this project.

ABOUT THE AUTHOR

Dr. Howard Kirschenbaum is co-founder of Sagamore Institute and was its Executive Director from 1971-1988. He is founder and President of Adirondack Architectural Heritage, the non-profit historic preservation organization for the Adirondack Park, and Vice-President of the Adirondack Nature Conservancy and Land Trust. His most recent project is the restoration of White Pine Camp near Saranac Lake, a unique "Great Camp" that served as President Coolidge's 1926 Summer White House, which he and his colleagues opened to the public in 1995 for historical and architectural tours.

Dr. Kirschenbaum is also an educator, international consultant on values and character education, and author of over twenty books in the fields of education, psychology and history. He may be reached at Box 130, Raquette Lake, NY 13436.

Historic Great Camp Sagamore is open to the public for a variety of educational and recreational programs throughout most of the year and for guided tours in the summer and fall.
For further information, write or call:

SAGAMORE INSTITUTE OF THE ADIRONDACKS
Sagamore Road
Raquette Lake, NY 13436
(315) 354-5303